D1563627

the little

LOVE

book

Hardie Grant

QUADRILLE

Love

Definition:
noun

1. An intense feeling of deep affection.
2. A strong feeling of affection and sexual attraction for someone.
3. Affectionate greetings conveyed to someone on one's behalf.
4. A formula for ending an affectionate letter.

Love

Definition:
verb

1. Feel deep affection for (someone).

2. Feel a deep romantic or sexual attachment to (someone).

3. Like or enjoy very much.

Gods of love

Eros (Greek)

Cupid (Roman)

Baldur (Norse)

Kama (Hindu)

Angus (Celtic)

Huehuecoyotl (Aztec)

Goddesses of love

Aphrodite (Greek)

Venus (Roman)

Hathor (Egyptian)

Freya (Norse)

Inanna (Sumerian)

Ishtar (Babylonian)

Rati (Hindu)

Astarte (Phoenician)

Aine (Celtic)

Xochiquetzal (Aztec)

"The force that unites the elements to become all things is Love, also called Aphrodite; Love brings together dissimilar elements into a unity, to become a composite thing. Love is the same force that human beings find at work in themselves whenever they feel joy, love and peace."

EMPEDOCLES

Empedocles, 490–430 BC was an Ancient Greek philosopher who cited love as being one of the vital forces that made up the universe.

The heart '♥' is the universal symbol of love

The palpitations, the throbbing, the skipping of a beat – the heart is the physical manifestation of love. It may seem obvious as it hammers, beats or flutters in your chest that the heart has become the universal symbol of love, but the actual organ is a fist-shaped muscle, not the symmetrical pretty shape that we all recognise.

Opinions vary as to when and why the heart shape first became irrevocably connected with love. Some suggest the shape is based on an ivy leaf, which represented fidelity or fennel bulbs, which were used as birth control, and others on the more carnal buttocks or breasts.

As a symbol of love, the heart became wildly popular in medieval Europe. It first made an appearance in a 13th century French romance (of course!), *Roman de la Poire* (*Romance of the Pear*) by Thibaut. In an exquisitely illuminated miniature of the letter S, a kneeling man hands his damsel the 'lover's heart'. From this tiny illustration flowed the trillions of hearts that decorate romantic cards the world over today.

While love cannot be conjured, gentle preparations can be made to ensure that when it does arrive you are able to offer it a warm embrace and a joyful home. Undertaking certain love seeking rituals can be the first step in undertaking the journey of love.

Peruvian upside down saints

In Catholic parts of Peru where small saints are kept as household icons, tradition dictates that when looking for love, the figurine of St. Anthony is turned upside down. When love is found, St. Anthony is placed upright once again.

Romania's Dragobete Day

Celebrated on 24th February in honour of Dragobete, a local Romanian god, this day of love sees young people head to the hills to pick flowers together. At noon, the girls run back to the village with the boys chasing behind. If a boy catches a girl and his love is reciprocated she will kiss him to make their love public. Today, tradition still suggests that if your love life is in the doldrums you can revive it simply by touching a member of the opposite sex on Dragobete's Day.

Modern deleting rituals

Frustrated by the ephemeral nature of digital love making, modern folk looking for love undertake the digital cleanse ritual. This involves deleting dating apps and previous lovers' contact details and deciding to engage fully with the offline world. Shunning online romance in favour of real-life connection is reputed to have some positive results.

Feng shui is the Ancient Chinese practice of using energy to harmonise spaces and people. The art of feng shui suggests you need to make the path clear for the energy qi, to flow smoothly between yourself and your lover.

Follow these simple feng shui prompts to welcome love into your soul:

- Don't wear a fringe: clear your forehead so qi can enter

- Wear red shoes: the festive colour red helps you walk towards love

- Embrace crimson bedsheets: sleep in a red bed and keep red threads under your pillow to bring good luck in love

*"Again love, the limb-loosener,
rattles me
bittersweet,
irresistible,
a crawling beast."*

SAPPHO

Make that romantic bouquet even more meaningful by understanding the language of flowers. The Royal Horticultural Society include these blooms as being particularly associated with love:

- Pink carnations – a woman's love

- Red chrysanthemum – I love you

- Forget-me-not – true love

- Garden pink (*Dianthus*) – pure love

- Yellow iris – flame of love

- Lavender – devotion

- Red tulip – declaration of love

Monogamous love is not simply a human endeavour, the *National Geographic* reports on the animals that mate for life:

• Prairie vole

• Gray wolf

• Macaroni penguin

• Lar gibbon

• Pot-bellied seahorse

• Black-necked swan

"After the division the two parts of man, each desiring his other half, came together, and throwing their arms about one another, entwined in mutual embraces, longing to grow into one... so ancient is the desire of one another which is implanted in us, reuniting our original nature, making one of two, and healing the state of man...And the reason is that human nature was originally one and we were a whole and the desire and pursuit of the whole is called love."

PLATO
Symposium

A soulmate is not found, it
is recognised, remembered.

"Love is a gift of one's innermost soul to another so both can be whole."

THE BUDDHA

"O heart,
there is no reality for me
other than she she
she she she
in the whole of the reeling world.
And philosophers talk about
Oneness."

AMARU SHATAKA

In 1979, psychologist Dorothy Tennov coined the term 'limerence' in her book *Love and Limerence: The Experience of Being in Love*. She describes an involuntary state of deep obsession and infatuation with another person.

Not to be confused with love, limerence is a state more akin to addiction. The state of limerence causes you to crave so deeply another person you lose focus on everything else in your life and suffer wild withdrawal symptoms if your affection is not reciprocated.

Mutual limerence creates intense intimate bonding and provides a passionate foundation for a cosy relationship. Explore whether it's love or limerence by asking yourself these questions:

1. Does your last interaction with the object of your affection merit the extreme euphoria it brought you?

2. Do your friends and family assess your 'relationship' in the same way you do?

3. Beyond how they make you feel, how much do you really know about the object of your limerence?

When falling in love with someone, your body is flooded with chemicals including norepinephrine, dopamine and phenylethylamine that produce feelings of euphoria.

Erotic love is a physiological phenomenon. Science textbooks, as well as the poetry of millennia, document the extreme physical changes that simultaneously electrify and incapacitate one in love.

Tick the number of physical symptoms you've experienced when in the throes of a love affair:

- Pulsating heart
- Throbbing genitals
- Sweaty palms
- Lurching stomach
- Flushing face

Love equals...

- Loss of appetite
- Sleeplessness
- Accelerated breathing
- Dilated pupils
- General restlessness
- Tingling spine

Love is like a fire. It needs to be continuously fed with the spark of joy, the ignition of passion, the oxygen of freedom and the fuel of continuous acts of loving kindness.

Love is...

- Never faking
- Letting them sleep in
- Holding hands without realising
- Respecting their privacy
- The delight at seeing them after an absence

To love is essential to life. We are born alone and immediately cry out our thirst for nourishment and affection. We need others both physically and emotionally. To live without the love of others is not to live at all.

Choose who you love wisely. Find a way to see clearly through the tumult of passion and ask yourself whether the object of your affection is decent as well as simply attractive. When the bonds of love are knotted from our heart to theirs, our happiness is tethered to their character.

"All our happiness or unhappiness depends on the quality of the object to which we are attached by love."

SPINOZA

Top 5 bestselling love ballads in the UK

1. 'Love is all around',
   Wet Wet Wet

2. 'Unchained melody',
   Robson and Jerome

3. '(Everything I do) I do it for you',
   Bryan Adams

4. 'Anything is possible / Evergreen',
   Will Young

5. 'I will always love you',
   Whitney Houston

Root your love by planting a
tree together:

- Crab apple: long associated with
  love, crab apples are also symbols
  of fertility

- Ash trees: offer protection, love
  and keep safe women's mysteries

- Hawthorn: perhaps because its
  wood burns the hottest, hawthorn
  protects love unions

Love takes the big stuff seriously

- Meeting the parents
- Remembering birthdays
- Moving in together
- Honouring commitments
- Discussing financial issues
- Turning up to family events
- Booking holidays
- Celebrating anniversaries
- Discussing children
- Supporting careers...

Being in a loving relationship means that the grinding cogs of life are well oiled and run smoothly.

In today's world, where we sometimes live far from our wider family, we have a tendency to expect everything of our partners.

Sit down with your partner and work out what loving services you are able to offer each other and where you need to outsource/hire support. Employing a cleaner, finding a reliable car mechanic or weekly fresh food delivery service, can do much to avoid frustrations with each other's perfectly human limitations. (Or move closer to your family!)

- Soulmate
- Lover
- Holiday planner
- Therapist
- Sounding board
- Decorator
- Plumber
- Cook
- Career advisor
- Care giver
- Cleaner
- Financial adviser...

Love does not need qualification

Love does not say, 'I will love you if...'

Love is...

- Two hearts that beat as one

- Four eyes that look in the same direction

- Two minds that think of each other

- Four legs that walk side by side

- Two mouths that join as one

Sometimes love falls in your lap like a gift from heaven.

Sometimes love grows from the most unpromising of bulbs.

Sometimes love is kneaded into life with warm hands and a burning heart.

Write a list of the first times shared with your partner. Really take yourself back to the moment shared and try to capture your feelings of early love.

- The first time we saw each other
- The first film we watched together
- The first meal we shared together
- The first time we kissed
- The first gifts we shared
- The first time we went away together
- The first time we said 'I love you'

Ovid, the Classical Latin poet in the age of Emperor Augustus wrote a wonderful self-help manual entitled: *Ars Amatoria* (*The Art of Love*). Offering advice on how to find and keep love, *Ars Amatoria* includes the invaluable advice to husbands as relevant then as now: do **not** forget your partner's birthday!

*"Love seeketh not itself to please,
Nor for itself hath any care, but for
Another gives its ease, and builds a
Heaven in Hell's despair."*

WILLIAM BLAKE

Sleeping with chamomile

Long used across Europe by those wishing to attract love, a chamomile sleep pillow is said to prepare your unconscious for love. Use either dried chamomile or make a little cotton bag and fill with chamomile flowers, place beneath your pillow, drift off to sleep and dream of your future love. In extremis, a chamomile teabag will also do the trick.

"Love is full of anxious fears."

OVID

The longest love story...

The current Guinness World Record for the world's longest marriage is between Herbert Fisher and Zelmyra (née George). They wed on 13 May 1924 and were married for 86 years and 290 days.

"*When marrying ask yourself this question: do you believe that you will be able to converse well with this person into your old age? Everything else in marriage is transitory.*"

NIETZSCHE

> *"Take away love and our earth is a tomb"*

ROBERT BROWNING

Elizabeth II is the British sovereign who has enjoyed the longest marriage in royal history. HM The Queen married Prince Philip on 20 November 1947, making their marriage at the time of publication, a remarkable 72 years long.

On their golden wedding anniversary in 1997, HM The Queen referred to her husband as 'My strength and stay'.

"We cease loving ourselves when no one loves us."

MADAME DE STAEL

Love is never invisible

Couples in love emit pulsing signals of their state for all the world to see: the sideways glance, the gentle brush of the collar, the uproarious laugh.

Three of the greatest love stories ever told...

- Ross and Rachel
- Bennett and Darcy
- Benedict and Beatrice

Over 10 seasons of *Friends*, from 1994–2004, the on/off love story between Ross and Rachel captivated the hearts of a generation. The gentle but uncertain palaeontologist Ross and the confident and friendly Rachel are obviously in love from their first meeting. Events, other lovers and each other, sabotage their romance, until the final episode when they both realise they are meant only for each other.

Jane Austen first named *Pride and Prejudice*, *First Impressions* as Elizabeth Bennett and Fitzwilliam Darcy entirely misread each other on first meeting. The aloof Darcy and the sparkling Elizabeth overcome class divides, awful families and their own stubbornness to find happiness in his huge country pile Pemberley.

A much more thoughtful and grown-up romance than Romeo and Juliet, *Much Ado About Nothing*, sees intelligent Benedict and Beatrice throw witty insults at each other. Their banter soon turns to love and after navigating various Shakespearian pitfalls, they marry and dance the play out.

"If our love is a sin, then heaven must be full of such tender and selfless sinning as ours."

RADCLYFFE HALL
The Well of Loneliness

Quarter of a million wedding bells a year

At the latest count in England and Wales in 2016, there was good news for older lovers: the age at which people are marrying continues to hit new highs as more and more over-50s tie the knot.

"By harmony the universe does move,
And what is harmony but mutual love?"

EARL OF ROCHESTER

However love arrives in your life, through arranged marriages, a dating app, a chance meeting, a blind date, the fundamental requirements of its flourishing are the same:

- Kindness

- Loyalty

- Fun

- Treats

- Security

- Eroticism

- And prosaically: a really comfortable sofa

"A very small degree of hope is sufficient to cause the birth of love."

STENDHAL
On Love

"He that never had sorrow of love, never had joy of it either!"

GOTTFRIED VON STRASSBURG

According to Gary Chapman in his 1992 book *The Five Love Languages* there are different ways of expressing and receiving love:

1. Receiving gifts
2. Spending quality time together
3. Words of affirmation
4. Acts of service
5. Physical touch

Understanding what motivates
both you and your lover within a
relationship can help the relationship
to flourish. Spend time with your
lover to discover which language of
love you can most easily translate.
If your lover responds best to words
of affirmation make sure you praise
them meaningfully and frequently. If
you respond well to spending quality
time together, make sure you diary in
regular date nights.

Love is like a pot plant: it needs both grubby roots and glorious blooms.

"*Love is patient, love is kind. It does not envy, it does not boast, it is not proud. It does not dishonour others, it is not self-seeking, it is not easily angered, it keeps no record of wrongs. Love does not delight in evil but rejoices with the truth. It always protects, always trusts, always hopes, always perseveres. Love never fails.*"

ST PAUL

Love is elemental

Love demands the fire of passion, the grounding of earth, the far horizons of air and the liberty of water.

Love can be found in the space between.

And in silence.

Love shines in hurtful words not uttered, in harsh actions not committed, in accusations not made.

One of the utter joys of a long-term loving relationship, is being reminded of tiny details from your own life that have flown from your mind.

Dedicate an afternoon to reminiscing with your loved one. Take a notebook and begin with your first holiday together. Your memories of shared experiences will vary and it's delightful to be reminded of events, feelings and details that have slipped your mind but lodged firmly in the memory bank of your loved one.

" The greatest happiness of life is the conviction that we are loved; loved for ourselves, or rather, in spite of ourselves."

VICTOR HUGO

Types of love

- Unconditional
- Romantic
- Affectionate
- Self-love
- Familiar
- Enduring
- Playful
- Obsessive

Catalysts of love

- The physical body
- The mind
- Memories
- Emotion
- Survival instinct
- Unconscious
- Soul
- Spirit

Drop a love bomb

Dedicate time to love bombing your loved one. It may feel counter-intuitive to attempt a love bomb when they are being crotchety or glum but that is when they most need your affection. Think entirely selflessly, rather than asking yourself 'What would we like to do together?' or 'What do we need?', ask yourself...

- What would they like to do alone?

- What would they like as a gift?

- How can I arrange this?

- What would make their eyes alight with pleasure?

Chocks away! Drop those love bombs!

5 gorgeous things every couple in love should try once

1. Kissing in the sea

2. Lying on a bank and watching the stars

3. Making love in every room in the house

4. Taking dancing lessons together

5. Writing love letters

5 sensible things every couple in love should do

1. Write a will

2. Keep screens out of the bedroom

3. Help each other stay healthy

4. Eat together

5. Respect the privacy of your relationship

"I was made and meant to look for you and wait for you and become yours forever."

ROBERT BROWNING

Love is a serious business: people's hearts are at stake. If you are in a loving relationship, act with kindness and integrity, be accountable. Learn too, to recognise whether your lover treats you with equivalent dignity.

"Men make love more intensely at 20, but make love better, however, at 30."

CATHERINE THE GREAT

"And what is a kiss, specifically? A pledge properly sealed, a promise seasoned to taste, a vow stamped with the immediacy of a lip, a rosy circle drawn around the verb 'to love'."

EDMOND ROSTAND
Cyrano de Bergerac

Love is a phoenix

Through the furnace of life's rough parts (illness, breakdown, disability, financial hardship), lovers gain strength and rise from the heat of fire, fortified, to soar on wings of love together.

Laughter is the soundtrack to love.

If it's making you sad, it's not love.

**Love cannot thrive
without forgiveness.**

Forgiving and being forgiven within
a loving relationship are like diving
into a pool on a scorching summer's
day: both essential and luxurious.

Go old school and print out text or WhatsApp messages. Bind these together and present them to your partner as your very own bundle of love letters.

Three unsent love letters were found amongst the papers of the genius Ludwig von Beethoven. Full of passion for a mysterious 'Immortal beloved' Beethoven never married. He signed all his letters romantically:

Eternally mine

Eternally yours

Eternally ours

Love is the ongoing validation
of one another.

"*Perhaps, after all, romance did not come into one's life with pomp and blare, like a gay knight riding down; perhaps it crept to one's side like an old friend through quiet ways; perhaps it revealed itself in seeming prose, until some sudden shaft of illumination flung athwart its pages betrayed the rhythm and the music, perhaps... perhaps... love unfolded naturally out of a beautiful friendship, as a golden-hearted rose slipping from its green sheath.*"

LUCY MAUD MONTGOMERY
Anne of Avonlea

Love is one of the great endeavours of life.

Scratch that.

Love is the great endeavour of life.

Love has the capacity to break egocentricity, crack narcissism and shatter self-absorption.

Don't mistake intensity of feeling with depth of love.

Romantic infatuation and long-term loving commitment are not mutually exclusive. While the wild fire of early love dies down, it need not go cold. Think of passionate infatuation as an ember that can be easily inflamed with decades worth of shared interests, laughter, romping (with each other), romantic gestures, loving words and yes, generous bouquets of flowers.

"I have no notion of loving people by halves, it is not my nature. My attachments are always excessively strong."

JANE AUSTEN
Northanger Abbey

Love is an endless conversation.

Love embellishes the simplest of pleasures. A cup of coffee tastes so much better when your lover is sitting opposite. A piece of toast has added crunch when your lover leans over to steal a bite. A long journey is made joyous when your lover winds down both windows and sings your song with you.

Top 10 romantic films

1. *Casablanca*, 1942
2. *It Happened One Night*, 1934
3. *The Shape of Water*, 2017
4. *Singin' in the Rain*, 1952
5. *The Big Sick*, 2017
6. *Call Me by Your Name*, 2018
7. *The Adventures of Robin Hood*, 1938
8. *Top Hat*, 1935
9. *The Philadelphia Story*, 1940
10. *Vertigo*, 1958

"Evil is the vulgar lover who loves the body rather than the soul, inasmuch as he is not even stable, because he loves a thing which is in itself unstable, and therefore when the bloom of youth which he was desiring is over, he takes wing and flies away, in spite of all his words and promises; whereas the love of the noble disposition is life-long, for it becomes one with the everlasting."

PLATO
Symposium

Love is the energy created when the spark of bodies ignites the union of two minds.

"Age does not protect you from love. But love, to some extent, protects you from age."

ANAÏS NIN

Rose; its scent, its colour, its beauty has been associated with love for as long as it has bloomed.

Rose quartz: known as the 'heart stone', the soft, feminine pink of rose quartz is said to inspire compassionate and loving energy.

Rose petals: the tears of Aphrodite and the blood of her lover Adonis mingled together and roses burst forth.

Rose bushes: a signifier of growing love.

The late 18th and early 19th century saw a group of men and women burst on to the artistic stage and place intensity of emotional experience above rational modernity.

Their names instantly conjure handsome figures brooding amidst stunning landscapes: Byron, Keats, Shelley etc.

Now known as the Romantics, the poetry they left behind is unsurpassed in its ability to capture the majesty of romantic feeling.

"Soul meets soul on lover's lips."

PERCY BYSSHE SHELLEY

"Love is my religion – I could die for that."

JOHN KEATS

"Love is the ultimate purpose of world history, the Amen of the universe."

NOVALIS

Love Hearts

For the taste of love simply reach for a packet of Love Hearts. The pastel coloured sweets have been made since 1933 by a British confectionary company. Share wisely!

Messages on the sweets are updated but currently include...

- All yours
- Be mine
- Call me
- Date me
- Dream on
- Email me
- Hot lips
- Kiss me
- New Love
- U rock
- You're mine

"For Nature is love, and finds haunts for true love,
Where nothing can hear or intrude;
It hides from the eagle and joins with the dove,
In beautiful green solitude."

JOHN CLARE

"The most powerful symptom of love is a tenderness which becomes at times almost insupportable."

VICTOR HUGO

"Thou demandest what is Love. It is that powerful attraction towards all we conceive, or fear, or hope beyond ourselves, when we find within our own thoughts the chasm of an insufficient void, and seek to awaken in all things that are, a community with what we experience within ourselves. If we reason, we would be understood; if we imagine, we would that the airy

children of our brain were born anew within another's; if we feel, we would that another's nerves should vibrate to our own, that the beams of their eyes should kindle at once and mix and melt into our own; that lips of motionless ice should not reply to lips quivering and burning with the heart's best blood. This is Love."

PERCY BYSSHE SHELLEY
'On Love'

" Who loves, raves."

LORD BYRON

"The bond of all companionship, whether in marriage or in friendship, is conversation."

OSCAR WILDE

"Love is enough: though the World be a-waning,
And the woods have no voice but the voice of complaining,
Though the sky be too dark for dim eyes to discover
The gold-cups and daisies fair blooming thereunder,
Though the hills be held shadows, and the sea a dark wonder,

*And this day draw a veil over all deeds,
pass'd over,
Yet their hands shall not tremble, their
feet shall not falter;
The void shall not weary, the fear shall
not alter
These lips and these eyes of the loved
and the lover."*

WILLIAM MORRIS
'Love is Enough'

"Love...interrupts at every hour the most precious occupations, and sometimes perplexes for a while even the greatest minds. It does not hesitate...to interfere with the negotiations of statesmen and the investigations of the learned. It knows how to slip its love-notes and ringlets even into ministerial portfolios and philosophical manuscripts... It sometimes demands the sacrifice of... health, sometimes of wealth, position and happiness."

ARTHUR SCHOPENHAUER

Love does not discriminate. Love throws into turmoil the rational, uplifts the pessimist, disrupts the orderly, brings uproar to the timid, makes silly the serious and brings joy to the lonely heart.

"Today, see if you can stretch your heart and expand your love so that it touches not only those to whom you can give it easily, but also to those who need it so much."

ARISTOTLE

"The capacity of loving is the largest of my powers."

ELIZABETH BARRETT BROWNING

"When myself is not with you, it is nowhere."

HÉLOÏSE

"*Cine Cerere et Baccho friget Venus*" –
this Latin maxim loosely translates as,
"love grows cold without food or wine."

Roses have been symbols of love since gardens have flowered and men have given posies to their lovers. Each colour rose has a specific meaning:

- Yellow: joyful love

- Red: passionate love

- Pink: true love

- White: innocence and purity

"Each time one loves is the only time one has ever loved."

OSCAR WILDE

" When one loves somebody everything is clear – where to go – what to do – it all takes care of itself and one doesn't have to ask anybody about anything."

MAXIM GORKY

The courtesy of love encourages us to speak kindly and act graciously to those we love.

If you wish to know whether someone loves you, listen to how they speak to you. If you wish to know whether you love someone, listen to how you speak to them.

Lust is the childhood of love.

To those we love:

- Encourage rather than correct
- Support rather than criticize
- Give suggestions not orders
- Critique the action, not the person

"For one human being to love another that is perhaps the most difficult of all our tasks, the ultimate, the last test and proof, the work for which all other work is but preparation."

RAINER MARIA RILKE

These books perfectly capture the sheer emotional tumult of being in love. Read at your peril, with tissues at the ready. Your heart will alight with joy and tremble in agony at these elegantly told stories of love.

1. *Persuasion*, Jane Austen

2. *Birdsong*, Sebastian Faulks

3. *The End of the Affair*, Graham Greene

4. *The Thorn Birds*, Colleen McCullough

5. *Dr Zhivago*, Boris Pasternack

Phrases for love

- For the love of God
- Love is blind
- Not for love or money
- Make love
- There's no love lost

Welsh love spoons

From the 17th century a lovely tradition
arose in Wales whereby young men
would carve spoons from a single
piece of wood to give to the girl he
loved. This tradition was ideal for shy
young boys who were uncomfortable
expressing their feelings in person but
could carve intricate hearts, wedding
bells and good luck horseshoes into
a spoon as a gift for the girl he loved.
The act of carving demonstrated to
the girl's father that the suitor was a
capable craftsman and thus able to
look after his daughter.

Welsh love spoons became more elaborate over the centuries and are still given as declarations of love.

Lenço do amor – Portuguese handkerchiefs of love

How to tell a boy you love them when you live in a socially conservative country such as Catholic Portugal was in times past? Young girls from Portugal would embroider delicate handkerchiefs and coyly present them to the object of their affection. If the feelings were reciprocated, the boy would wear the brightly decorated handkerchief in his jacket pocket at church. The Portuguese handkerchiefs of love, more often embroidered by older village ladies, can still be bought at heritage craft stalls.

Famous love lock locations:

1. Most Ljubavi, Bridge of Love in Vrnjačka Banja, Serbia

2. Pont des Arts, Paris

3. Brooklyn Bridge, New York

4. Hohenzollern Bridge, Cologne

5. North Seoul Tower, Seoul

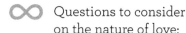 Questions to consider
on the nature of love:

- Does trying to define love
de-nature it?

- Does describing love as this,
or that, undermine it?

- Do efforts to categorise love
destroy love's ephemeral nature?

- Can you bring rationality to love?

- Should love only live in the realm
of feeling?

"To love someone is to identify with them."

ARISTOTLE

Freudian thinking explains love in terms of regression. Every human has a deep memory of the sheer bliss and perfect safety of being at their mother's breast. Love therefore seeks to recreate this remembered feeling of utter love and devotion.

"As I got to know you, I began to realise that beauty was the least of your qualities. I became fascinated by your goodness. I was drawn in by it. I didn't understand what was happening to me. And it was only when I began to feel actual, physical pain every time you left the room that it finally dawned on me: I was in love, for the first time in my life. I knew it was hopeless, but that didn't matter to me. And it's not that I want to have you. All I want is to deserve you. Tell me what to do. Show me how to behave. I'll do anything you say."

CHODERLOS DE LACLOS
Dangerous Liaisons

141

Love allows us to discover our inner world through a relationship with another. Love allows us to actualise our potential.

Love unleashes tremendous desire to give to the other. With love at your disposal all manner of obstacles can be overcome, for love is a force unlike any other.

"*They loved each other, not driven by necessity, by the 'blaze of passion' often falsely ascribed to love. They loved each other because everything around them willed it, the trees and the clouds and the sky over their heads and the earth under their feet. Perhaps their surrounding world, the strangers they met in the street, the wide expanses they saw on their walks, the rooms in which they lived or met, took more delight in their love than they themselves did.*"

BORIS PASTERNAK
Dr Zhivago

144

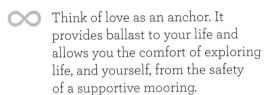 Think of love as an anchor. It provides ballast to your life and allows you the comfort of exploring life, and yourself, from the safety of a supportive mooring.

Is love unconditional?

Should love really survive betrayal, infidelity, abuse? If we set too much store by the unconditionality of love are we burdening our relationships with expectations that will ultimately undermine them?

"Love is like the measles. The older you get it, the worse the attack."

RAINER MARIA RILKE

Love is...

- Sharing your pudding when they insisted they were 'full' and hadn't ordered their own

- Asking for two spoons

- Only using one

With their luscious red flesh, pomegranates were used by the Ancient Greeks to make an aphrodisiac wine. Also known as 'apples of love', a bagful of pomegranates would make a charming gift for a lover. Tear open and devour the ruby red seeds (or indeed each other).

Love is...

- The space between you and the mutual desire for it to evaporate
- The tender kiss afterwards
- Trust in their absence
- Holding them all night
- Being held all night

"As love is the most noble and divine passion of the soul, so is it that to which we may justly attribute all the real satisfactions of life, and without it, man is unfinished, and unhappy."

APHRA BEHN

Exquisitely beautiful and witty, Ninon de L'Enclos, 1620–1705, was a French courtesan and author. During her long life she witnessed great social changes in France, which gave her a grounded understanding of matters of the heart.

*"Love without desire is a delusion:
it does not exist in nature."*

NINON DE L'ENCLOS

Love is...

- Cooking their favourite meal
- Comfortable silence
- Doing the bins
- A place of safety

*"Life is too short to be able
to love as one should."*

QUEEN CHRISTINA OF SWEDEN

"You can give without loving but you can never love without giving."

ROBERT LOUIS STEVENSON

Love is more than an emotion; it is a way of life. To be in love with someone does not simply mean you've lost your appetite and hunger for nothing more than their presence. Rather, to love, is to carry out endless acts of loving kindness. And to be loved is to be the recipient of endless acts of loving kindness.

To love and to be loved is to create your own eternal circle of mutual love.

Think not of love as a diamond: beautiful, precious, but unchanging. Think instead of love as a sourdough starter: messy but fizzing with life.

Feed your love, care for it tenderly and with two hands together, knead your love into a delicious loaf of love that nourishes you both throughout life.

Though an adventure, love is more akin to feeling at home. Love makes you feel you've arrived at where you have always meant to be.

Intentional loving idea

Begin each day by alighting on one act of love to complete before the day's end.

An act of love for your heart's desire can be as small as messaging them a few kisses to as flamboyant as booking a surprise romantic getaway. Whatever the action, the act must be motivated by love.

Love's golden key is **trust**; without it, hearts will never open.

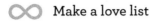 **Make a love list**

Find somewhere beautiful to sit.

Bring a notebook and a pen and fill your mind with the one you love.

Write down all the reasons you love them, including the simplest details – that tiny freckle behind their ear, and the biggest – how they spoke to your mum when they first met, for instance.

Keep your loving list somewhere close and don't forget to keep adding to your list as you continue on love's path together.

There are various contrasting relationships that will be inhabited within a long-term committed romance. Your relationship will transfigure from one to another while retaining its essential foundations.

When embarking on the loving journey of your life, expect your relationship to appear in many guises. From the first relationship of euphoric pair bonding, to co-dependency, parenthood, the bearer of the other, the party being carried, world travellers, the example to future generations.

Love is...

- Making the bed every morning
- An unnecessary box of chocolates
- Taking it in turns to comfort your poorly child in the dim hours before dawn
- Unloading the shopping from the car boot
- Catching each other's eye in a crowded room

"*Love participates of the soul itself. It is of the same nature. Like it, it is the divine spark; like it, it is incorruptible, indivisible, imperishable. It is a point of fire that exists within us, which is immortal and infinite, which nothing can confine, and which nothing can extinguish. We feel it burning even to the very marrow of our bones, and we see it beaming in the very depths of heaven...*"

VICTOR HUGO
Les Misérables

"Each moment of a happy lover's hour is worth an age of dull and common life."

APHRA BEHN

"I have for the first time found what I can truly love — I have found you. You are my sympathy — my better self — my good angel; I am bound to you with a strong attachment. I think you are good, gifted, lovely: a fervent, a solemn passion is conceived in my heart; it leans to you, draws you to my centre and spring of life, wraps my existence about you — and, kindling in pure, powerful flame, fuses you and me in one."

CHARLOTTE BRONTË
Jane Eyre

"Love is not a hot-house flower, but a wild plant, born of a wet night, born of an hour of sunshine; sprung from wild seed, blown along the road by a wild wind. A wild plant that, when it blooms by chance within the hedge of our gardens, we call a flower; and when it blooms outside we call a weed; but, flower or weed, whose scent and colour are always, wild!"

JOHN GALSWORTHY
The Forsyte Saga

"Oh, what a love it was, utterly free, unique, like nothing else on earth! Their thoughts were like other people's songs."

BORIS PASTERNAK
Dr Zhivago

To see the power of love beyond death, only visit any graveyard, anywhere in the world. There, etched in stone are words of love about ordinary people whose lives have touched another.

Epitaphs from a village graveyard:

"As a light shines in the darkness, from you came the only brightness of my life."

"The light of my life. The joy of my soul. Joined again in eternity."

"To have loved you was enough."

Love is fusion: two souls forever forged together. Think Romeo and Juliet or Heathcliff and Catherine in *Wuthering Heights*, finally joined together in death.

The most powerful depiction of love as fusion can be found in the medieval story of Tristan and Isolde. Even when their love causes tragedy, it cannot be denied, and the lovers eventually die as one.

"They both laughed and drank to each other; they had never tasted sweeter liquor in all their lives. And in that moment they fell so deeply in love that their hearts would never be divided. So the destiny of Tristan and Isolde was ordained."

SIR THOMAS MALORY

To experience the capacious fury of love, listen to Wagner's *Tristan and Isolde*. Its chromatic dissonance captures perfectly the ecstasies and agonies of a love that cannot be denied.

The libretto of *Tristan and Isolde* where the lovers fuse into one, reads not unlike modern Instagram poetry.

TRISTAN
"Tristan you,
I Isolde,
No longer Tristan!"

ISOLDE
"You Isolde,
Tristan I,
No longer Isolde!"

TOGETHER
"Un-named,
Free from parting
New perception,
New enkindling;
Even endless
Self-knowing;
Warmly glowing heart,
Love's utmost joy!"

Some love stories are so potent that though both participants have passed away their love leaves a legacy that we can enjoy today.

The Eleanor Crosses are a series of 12 crosses raised by Edward I in memory of his much beloved wife Eleanor of Castille who died in 1290. Tall and elegantly decorated, the stone crosses mark the route of her funerary procession from Lincoln to London.

The Taj Mahal is an unparalleled monument to love. Constructed by the Mughal Emperor Shah Jahan, the exquisite mausoleum, entombs his beloved third wife Mumtaz Mahal.

The Albert Memorial is a virile monument raised in 1872 by Queen Victoria to honour her deceased husband. Replete with wrought iron work and gold filigree the monument celebrates Albert's passionate interest in arts and science. It is hard also to ignore its rather phallic proportions indicative of the lively bedroom scene Victoria and Albert were said to have enjoyed.

Mitchell and Cam in *Modern Family*

Replete with bickering, family over-involvement, career ups and downs, Mitchell Pritchett and Cameron Tucker are the essence of modern in the long-running mockumentary *Modern Family*. First aired in 2009, the programme goes beyond the happy ending to show how true love, of whatever stripe, thrives in the muddle of family life. The love Mitchell and Cam, who together raise their adopted daughter Lily, have for each other, deepens as their family matures.

Love accepts the flaws
in those whom we love.

Adam and Ian in *The Archers*

Adam Macy, the rugged farmer, and Ian Craig, the sociable chef, shared their first kiss in a strawberry field together in 2004. Their relationship has beamed through the airwaves of BBC Radio 4's *The Archers*, the longest running drama in the world. Now married and fathers to baby Xander, Adam and Ian's loving relationship sits at the beating heart of the show.

Maurice and Alec in *Maurice*

Written circa 1914, *Maurice* by
E. M. Forster was only published
posthumously in 1971. In this achingly
beautiful coming of age novel, Forster
depicts their love story as sensual,
feeling and ultimately inevitable.
The happy ever after ending, where
they escape to the countryside to live
together is poignant beyond measure.

Carol and Therese in *Carol*

Based on Patricia Highsmith's 1952 novel *The Price of Salt*, *Carol* is the 2015 shimmering film of forbidden love starring Cate Blanchett and Rooney Mara. It's the smile that reveals all. The final scene where Therese finally walks towards a waiting Carol, their eyes meet and a smile shows everything.

"*I cannot alter – my affection and love is beyond even this world! Nothing will shake it but yourself; and that I will not allow myself to think for a moment is possible.*"

LORD NELSON
Letters of Lord Nelson to Lady Hamilton

QUOTES ARE TAKEN FROM

Amaru Shataka, 9th century Sanskrit poet

Anaïs Nin, 20th century American writer

Aphra Behn, 17th century English writer

Arthur Schopenhauer, 19th century German philosopher

Aristophanes, Ancient Greek philosopher

Boris Pasternak, 20th century Russian writer

Catherine the Great, Empress of Russia

Catullus, Roman poet

Charlotte Brontë, 19th century English author

Choderlos de Laclos, 18th century French author

Christina, 17th century Queen of Sweden

Earl of Rochester, 17th century English poet

Edmond Rostand, 19th century French dramatist

Elizabeth Barrett Browning, 19th century English writer

Empedocles, Ancient Greek philosopher

Geoffrey Chaucer, 14th century English author

Gottfried von Strassburg, 12th century German poet

Hafız, 14th century Persian poet

Héloïse, 12th century French nun

Henry Fielding, 18th century English author

Jane Austen, 18th century English novelist

John Clare, 19th century English poet

John Donne, 16th century English poet

John Galsworthy, 20th century English author

John Keats, early 19th century English poet

Lord Byron, 19th century English writer

Lord Nelson, 19th century English naval hero

Louisa May Alcott, 19th century American author

Lucy Maud Montgomery, 20th century
Canadian author

Madame de Staël, 18th century Franco-Swiss
woman of letters

Maxim Gorky, 20th century Russian writer

Friedrich Nietzsche, 19th century German
philosopher

Ninon de L'Enclos, 17th century French writer and
courtesan

Novalis, 18th century German writer

Oscar Wilde, 19th century Irish poet
and playwright

Ovid, Roman poet

Percy Bysshe Shelley, 19th century English writer

Peter Abelard, 12th century French monk

Plato, Ancient Greek philosopher

Radclyffe Hall, 20th century English writer

Rainer Maria Rilke, 20th century Bohemian-Austrian poet

Robert Browning, 19th century English poet and playwright

Robert Louis Stevenson, 19th century Scottish writer

Sappho, Ancient Greek poet

Sir Thomas Malory, 14th century English author and poet

Somerset Maugham, 20th century English author

Baruch Spinoza, 17th century Dutch philosopher

Stendhal (aka Marie-Henri Beyle), 19th century French writer

St Paul, founding father of the Christian church

Victor Hugo, 19th century French author

William Blake, 19th century English poet, painter and visionary

William Morris, 19th century poet, novelist and textile designer

BIBLIOGRAPHY AND FURTHER READING

A History of Western Philosophy,
Bertrand Russell, 1946

Encyclopaedia Britannica, 1768

Essays in Love, Alain de Botton, 2015

Love, A History, Simon May, 2011

Love and Limerence, Dorothy Tennov, 1972

Love Letters of Great Men and Women From the 18th Century to the Present Day, C. H. Charles, 1924

On Love, Henri Stendhal, Penguin Classics, 1995

Ovid, The Love Poems, Oxford World Classics, 2008

Oxford Dictionary of Quotations, 1941

Midsummer; Rituals, Recipes and Lore for Litha, Deborah Blake, 2015

The Five Love Languages, Gary Chapman, 1992

The Four Loves, C. S. Lewis, 1960

The New Penguin Book of Romantic Poetry, 2005

The Oxford Book of English Verse, 1999

The Reader's Handbook, The Reverend E. Cobham Brewer, 1895

The Poems of Catullus, Oxford World Classics, 2008

The Symposium, Plato, Penguin Classics, 2003

Sufi Poems, A Mediaeval Anthology, 2004

USEFUL WEBSITES

Archive.org

Britannica.com

Oxforddnb.com

Scholar.google.com

Officialcharts.com

Publishing Director Sarah Lavelle
Assistant Editor Stacey Cleworth
Words Joanna Gray
Series Designer Emily Lapworth
Junior Designer Alicia House
Head of Production Stephen Lang
Production Controller Sinead Hering

Published in 2020 by Quadrille,
an imprint of Hardie Grant
Publishing

Quadrille
52–54 Southwark Street
London SE1 1UN
quadrille.com

The publisher has made every
effort to trace the copyright
holders. We apologize in advance
for any unintentional omissions
and would be pleased to insert the
appropriate acknowledgement in
any subsequent edition.

Cataloguing in Publication Data:
a catalogue record for this book is
available from the British Library.

ISBN 978 1 78713 611 3

Printed in China